Home After the Maple

Hassan A. J.

BookLeaf Publishing

Presentation by *BookLeaf Publishing*

Web: www.bookleafpub.com

E-mail: info@bookleafpub.com

ISBN: 9789357613316

First edition 2023

DEDICATION

for those who'd kept on writing & those who will

ACKNOWLEDGEMENT

A special thanks to
my family,
Darla,
Max,
Mina,
Kevin,
Florian,
& Harry

PREFACE

I didn't
always know that apocalypse

meant not the end of the world but
the universe disclosing its knowledge

as the sea is meant to give up its dead,
the big reveal, when the veil blows back
                    --RebeccaLindenberg

                And How did I
        get back? How did any of us
        get back when we searched
                for beauty?
                        --Gary SOTO

Poems Made of Plagued Maple

My old poems resurface like a locked
chest in my chest. *Where have you been?*

they ask. You tend to forget to tend
to your sorrow until it belts out of your pen's

throat. Until it spills in the night staining
a stranger's tongue. Your name spelled out

in letters far from your mother tongue. Letters
erase the alphabet of your birth & replace

the word FRUIT with FOREIGN.
My old poems are planted in rabbit bone's

dust, in mulch and manure
at a still garden as the world stood still

in the hills of a green state
two years away from the chest

of a man from the garden state.
My old poems are spoken word

spoken when a firefly died on my window

-sill, where a bee mistook my room

for a hive. My old poems are made of plagued
maple labeled Higher Education, where Fine

Arts' finest frauds are cradled. Now—
In the distance of mountain from shore

I can stand / on this summit and watch
words once stomached   breathe

Leaves / Of Grass

When the scholar climbed a mountain
in Vermont, a Gulf parted
the water shimmered and stirred its ships
out of his mouth

What did history say
about strangers in strange
lands? About palm fronds
in fields of maple. About foreign
tongues accustomed to nor'easters
and flurries

When the scholar climbed the maple
tree its bark bent his back to its shape
His shape   a print against leaves

Of grass   he knew only
what the spears had shown

What Happened in Montpelier?

She says that the narrative
I tell myself becomes
the reality I live. Words
compounded by a shovel's
crunch
        thwack
            thud

When we dug up a garden
on that hill, we made a grave.
Or did we plant a cemetery
and watched a forest sprout?

Maybe we fostered our tar
-scented fears, lost sight
of our tangerine-colored hopes
& dreams.

But I only know how to speak
in Stone, so I tell her
what I know:
        That a stone
            scraped by the ocean
          is shaped
                    after its waves

Introspection in the Time of COVID

Sound[1] / sound[2] / sound[3] / sound[4] / sound[5] / sound[6] / sound[7] / sound[8]

Listen—it was never about the microscopic
viral particles in the air itself;
but about the mirrors
we stood before,
listening to glistening   scabs
that never healed.

How long has it been
since I've had this diagonal

                            scar
                 running up my left ribs
                      across my

collarbone

                                          &

along my neck,
                      hiding

behind my ears?

----

[1]The hum of the fridge [2]A tin can trapped in an alley spinning in the wind [3]Fiona Apple's bolt cutters [4]The owls migrating south [5]folklore & evermore [6]A muted zoom call [7]Interlude ii to 911 [8]Your own voice at seven

"wedge-shaped core of
darkness"

For what it's worth
self-worth is the only
needle in a compass

pointing a body towards
a body, towards a garden,
towards a war.

An index points at a body's
mouth. The tip of a shovel
points at a ground to plant.
A rifle points at an uncharted
land to map.

We were born with parts
in tarp bags and no IKEA
manual, spent our days
and nights assembling our
reflections.

I write
this poem riding
towards   my own name

The Sky is (Not) Falling

Generalized Anxiety Disorder is
a mother   calling
a homeland's embassy
in a foreign land   searching
for a son

The etymology of catastrophe is
simple: a son's neck purple with
grief / constricted by a monster's
grip / the son's eyes are gouged
out by claws / of godless pharaohs
in falcon masks / the son's skull
is trapped / between concrete
and rubber / Or maybe / he's
standing over a cracked glacier/
chasm / widening between
his feet

The son—may or may not—
walk through the front door
scars lost in translation. Color—
may or may not—fill the mother's
face once again. & shrapnel
of a fallen sky—may or may not—float
back   above the sun

Suffice

With a box of Truly and a ton of Taco Bell
she camped with a stranger in a trailer made
for two.   Their third was a dog, Tera, who
sniffed her edges inspecting their sudden union.
They Met on Tinder   a swipe leading to a bon-
fire   a swipe leading to the bottom of a
winebottle the cork sizzling to a crisp under the
maple trees. Estranged, and part of a strange
field unable to escape the borders of the state
as death toll covered their screens. In that state
she learned that dogs nest as she watched
Tera build her own bed   cradle its edges with
blankets and pillows make do with what heaven
hands. In a trailer the size of a litterbox destitute
dogs clench every spark of serotonin between
their teeth

Russian Doll of Perception

A FRAME

Here is a field of green slopes where an Irish
Setter roam grazing blades of grass with his
copper-colored muzzle. Here is god's
blue-colored ceiling, earth's hat sprinkled with
cotton. An index and a thumb hover over the
field, zoom in and out, pixels trapped in a black
frame the size of a bar of soap

A FRAME

Birds don't chirp in pictures of charged batteries
and light. But the woman in a wine-stained
bathrobe can hear it—an auditory conjuring of a
past existence, before the doors were sealed
shut, before her fingers smelled of ethanol and
isopropanol

A FRAME

An olfactory firing cannot register from motion
pictures trapped in a black frame the size of an
Edward Munch painting. With a click, you turn
the TV off. And with it, dimmed were the fields
of green and the dog, and the woman + her grape
stains of a costume on a Hollywood set.

Valedictorians of the In-between

Let's start med school again   after
our white coat ceremony.   Let's
learn once more how to spare
a life. How to avoid the carotid
when performing a tracheotomy.
How to angle a needle to a body's
rivers of blood

Let's do it over and over and over
master and remaster a trade
Students   forever   our status
on earth is *becoming / still / work-
in-progress / residents of purgatory*
practicing for the real world's heaven

When buried in textbooks is unbearable
let's bury our bodies   in flesh
quench a bloodsucker's thirst, bare
our necks   both carotid an offering

Don't tell us to board a flight
home when soil blooms. Don't
tell us to bathe in the silence
of fathers whose eyes a skill

we'll never master

We   cross-continental astronauts
with graves in our rearview mirrors
still becoming   working to progress
Spinning in flamed hoops with no halos
Waiting   for a glimpse of heaven

ii

(dis)order

Don't
(let the crows
nesting
in your head
write the day)

Introduction to Craft

Crafting a body is crafting a poem / the
architecture of prose is the construction of
monuments / words / the building blocks of a
body / the cells / the sap / the atoms / the helix
strands knitted before the self / become the body
/ become the self / a pen's ink / a neuron's spark
/ a squid's spit / a poet in a chair / a table pressed
against a window / a mother—/ a mother's legs
spread wide open / godhood / an architect / a
maker / a creator / a caretaker / a monument /
monumental / pain illuminating / a body crafting
another body / hands knitting a cloth in which a
self is swaddled / light from a window / a poet's
lamp / a mother's lap /   a chair /
a table /   ink /   a
self/   a body/   a poem

Lessons in Poetry

Hold on a minute
& look—tell me
how the fields
in your mind look.
The initial spark of
poetry is smoke
out of a forest
out of a chimney
out of a tucked
away house.
Start with the house
& then the thoughts
you house.
The valence shell &
then the atom. Split
the atom open and let
the coiled DNA spill,
the reader picking up
strands off the ground
like scattered pills.
Don't spell
your sleeves out,
only the texture
& a hint of the color.
The shape will rise

like oven-baked
strands from your life.

What I'm asking
you to do is turn
the raw pictures
into art.

When well versed, flip
the geometry
of your ink outwards;
valence shell to inward
atom bottled like
a cure in print.

i.e
a blond eyelash disappearing in spears
of black hair on your forearm
i.e
a broken bone mending inside a forearm

i.e
the perfume bottle your mother gifted
you unaware that the scent belongs to
an ex-lover whose loss you were still
grieving

Revision

Here is an overgrown
tree in full bloom.
Watch where you cut
the branches. Don't
tell me that the bruise
is purple. And don't
dance with the *s*
sound long
after the fair.
Remember—
what's worse
than cliché
is monotony.
Voice & meaning
braided. One
borrowed,
the other
birthed.
Make the reader
taste the sound
of a cracked hip
as if watching
a child tugged out
of a mother.
Mother your

pronouns & time
with care.
A cause—
a cause is what
every leaf must
sprout for

a poem without a body

Let's begin this painting
with a body in a body
of water   endless
ink
          smeared
                    along the canvas

Let's end this poem
with its colors   bottled
in barrels   language
a currency
               spent
                    on serotonin

The Lines

and life
is only a poem we write
old drafts
     remain printed on the page

iii

U- Haul

There was the glass house on the desert road /
and there was the red-bricked room above the
bar of a new haven / then there was the crescent
view of a foreign hill / followed / by the eclipsed
town on a forgotten mountain

On Wisconsin Avenue I began to patch the scars
/ of Mount Carmel and Temple Street / but I was
left / with the ghost of College Street / its
lampposts flickering in my head / its song
echoing in my footsteps

How did we rid ourselves of the sirens / in
rearview mirrors / when we were blind/folded
behind the wheel of a U-Haul / stuck on a
highway / towards tomorrow

stoned at the end of the world
as the world ends

I rode a wild horse once
in a field of fluorescent light
as gemstones latched
on to my blood cells
and galloped along the halls
of my veins

What I'm trying to say is—
I knew ecstasy once. Rolled
her edges and watched the clock
roll

The rush spilled out of a dealer's
sachet like a thumb scrolling past
narcotics

I see the name of the game in
pink neon signs spelled

in many fonts. We coped—
& reality filtered through the blur
of Instagram filters

Somewhere—a weathervane spun

& an upstairs neighbor sang

25

Home After the Maple

I only exist in digits—in the pixels
I scroll past, in the poems I pray

I exist in the lines of books, in letters
curved along the shape of my parietal

bone. I exist in the song. in the crumbs
of melodies lodged between my teeth.

That second week of March I stopped
existing in the world, in the air surrounding

every inch of my skin. I turned inward,
 like a shore reseeding, like birth in reverse,

 like a Sequoia shrinking back
 into the folds of a seed.

That second week of March I drove up
to the mountain, to a hideaway

from the air itself. That second
week of March I was barred

behind my eyelashes watching shutters
turn to trapdoors. I am learning—

I am learning how to exist
in this world again. My hideaway

behind me, a mountain framed
in a rearview mirror.

I am relearning what I once knew
a knowledge tossed out of the

passenger side window, somewhere
along the tracks of my twenties,

somewhere beneath the sand of 2020.
I am learning how to spell inward with air,

how to spring words out of my throat, how
to hold someone else's gaze and how

to finally toss my mask aside and speak.
I am practicing how to spit melodies

into my palm and set them free

30

Every ending took
something   someone's
back   turning

I stand   watching
the Golden Gate's flames
light the way

BLUE / HONEY

This is a LIGHT BLUE,
OVAL-shaped TABLET
imprinted with I | G on the
front and 213 on the
back

This is a tablet the color
of the spine of Didion's
Year of Magical Thinking, vintage
edition

May it rest on your tongue
and melt like blue honey, pixels
of white flags in a field of death
drowned out by "PURE/HONEY"

May your eyes blaze like gemstones
OBSIDIAN igniting sparks
& Himalayan Blue Poppy
climb your spine

What was it like being trapped
behind your eyelashes? Windows
barred shut, a neighbor's
exhale spelling coffin

What was it like in ancient
Greece when no word spelled
blue? Persephone, standing
beneath oval-shaped clouds
unable to palette black
from blue

Honey—you stood on the back
of a year drowning in drought
Your tongue   a raft and now
you're here   Open your mouth
and taste   the clouds

H

And in the final count
-down I must   count
my blessings

I must list all the rays
of light that shined
in spite of the concrete

You   stroke my hair
and tell me, "In the grand
scheme of things   pain
is nothing   but a snail
climbing a pebble"

So I count—
   I count your *every*
      single
freckle

9 789357 613316